CONTENTS

WHAT'S THE PROBLEM?

Most adults are kind and loving to children. But sometimes adults hurt children or make them feel bad. They may say cruel things to children and never show them the affection they need to feel loved. They may kick, beat or punch them. They may **neglect** them by leaving them at home alone for long periods of time, not give them enough to eat, or clothes to keep warm. Or they may touch them in a way that makes the child feel worried or unhappy.

CHILD ABUSE

When an adult treats a child like this it is called child **abuse**. Child abuse is not about getting told off now and then, or not being given exactly what you want. Child abuse is about an adult treating a child badly most or even all of the time, making that child feel unloved and that their feelings are not important. Or it may happen occasionally but be so damaging that it has lasting effects. There may be reasons why an adult hurts a child. The adult may have problems of their own, or have been badly treated themselves when they were young. But whatever the reason, child abuse is always wrong, the child is never to blame for the abuse and the abuse must always be stopped.

Abuse can damage children's lives for years. They need help to recover from their suffering. Sometimes they need *counselling* right through to their adult years.

Michael has a violent father. He has often been kicked and punched as well as being beaten with a belt. As well as bruising his body, the abuse has hurt his feelings and damaged his confidence too.

4

At least one child under five dies each week in the UK as a result of cruelty.

LOUISE SPILSBURY

www.heinemann.co.uk
Visit our website to find out more information about **Heinemann Library** books.

To order:
 Phone 44 (0) 1865 888066
Send a fax to 44 (0) 1865 314091
Visit the Heinemann Bookshop at www.heinemann.co.uk to browse our catalogue and order online.

First published in Great Britain by Heinemann Library, Halley Court, Jordan Hill, Oxford OX2 8EJ, a division of Reed Educational and Professional Publishing Ltd. Heinemann is a registered trademark of Reed Educational & Professional Publishing Limited.

OXFORD MELBOURNE AUCKLAND JOHANNESBURG BLANTYRE
GABORONE IBADAN PORTSMOUTH NH (USA) CHICAGO

Designed by Ken Vail Graphic Design, Cambridge
Originated by Universal Colour Scanning
Printed by Wing King Tong in Hong Kong

Heinemann Library paid a contribution to National Society for the Prevention of Cruelty to Children for their help in the creation of this book.

ISBN 0 431 02736 6 (hardback)   ISBN 0 431 02742 0 (paperback)
05 04 03 02 01   05 04 03 02 01
10 9 8 7 6 5 4 3 2 1   10 9 8 7 6 5 4 3 2 1

British Library Cataloguing in Publication Data
Spilsbury, Louise
National Society for the Prevention of Cruelty to Children (NSPCC). – (Taking Action!)
1.National Society for the Prevention of Cruelty to Children – Juvenile literature
I.Title
361.7'63'0941

Acknowledgements
The Publishers would like to thank the NSPCC for supplying all the photographs used in this book, except p30 (Corbis).

Cover illustration by Scott Rhodes.

Our thanks to staff at National Society for the Prevention of Cruelty to Children for their help in the preparation of this book.

Every effort has been made to contact copyright holders of any material reproduced in this book. Any omissions will be rectified in subsequent printings if notice is given to the Publisher.

The cases used in this book are real. Details have been disguised to preserve the identity of the people involved. The adults and children appearing in the photographs are models.

Words appearing in the text in bold, **like this**, are explained in the Glossary.

Lucy's mum leaves her alone for long periods of time, while she goes out to work. Lucy finds it lonely and scary to be left alone. It is also dangerous – there are a lot of safety risks in a house for a curious, exploring child.

Around 150–200 children die in England and Wales every year after being abused or neglected.

THE NSPCC THEN AND NOW

Can you imagine a dog or a cat having more **rights** than you? In the early 1880s this was the situation for children in the United Kingdom. There were laws to protect animals, but not children. Many children all over the country were suffering cruelty and **neglect** but there was little anyone could really do about it.

HELPING CHILDREN

Then, in 1883, a banker called T. F. Agnew set up the Liverpool Society for the Prevention of Cruelty to Children. He had been impressed by a similar organization he had seen on a trip to New York, USA, and wanted to help the children of his own city in the same way. By 1884 there was a children's society in London led by a minister, Reverend Benjamin Waugh. Under Waugh's guidance, this society pushed for the first **Act of Parliament** for the Prevention of Cruelty to Children, which was passed in 1889. In the same year the different groups which had sprung up around the country united into a national society – the National Society for the Prevention of Cruelty to Children, or NSPCC.

In the 1880s many children lived under appalling conditions – suffering cruel treatment from drunken parents, sent to work for long hours, left to beg in the streets, often cold and starving and without any hope of seeing a doctor when they became ill.

Benjamin Waugh was one of the most important people in the early days of the NSPCC. He was determined to draw public and government attention to the needs of children who had no one else to speak for them.

The NSPCC's goal is to end cruelty to children.

NSPCC TODAY

Today the NSPCC is the largest independent organization in Britain that specializes in child protection and the prevention of cruelty to children. The **charity** has been working for over 100 years to help children all over the country. There are teams of people all over England, Northern Ireland and Wales who work together and with families, communities and other organizations to end cruelty to children.

TOSH, AGE 3.
10 w, normal 274.3 oz

▲ The first NSPCC inspectors were known as 'Cruelty Men' because it was their job to save children from cruelty. Cruelty Men were good at talking to children and dealing politely with family members, but forceful enough to act firmly to help the children.

▶ The greatest reward for anyone who works for the NSPCC or donates money to help it carry out its work must be the smiling faces of children whose lives have been improved with the charity's help.

There are 156 NSPCC teams and projects throughout England, Wales and Northern Ireland.

WHAT DOES THE NSPCC DO?

The NSPCC works to put a stop to all cruelty to all children. As well as helping individual children through its projects in England, Wales and Northern Ireland, it works to help all children by **campaigning** to encourage everyone to put children's needs first.

LOCAL PROJECTS

The NSPCC teams across the country work in lots of different ways. There are regional units that carry out investigations into possible cases of **abuse**. There are family centres where families can go for advice and support, and children can play.

Anyone can ring the NSPCC telephone Helpline. The call is free and the phone line is open 24 hours a day, every day of the year.

Children are at the heart of everything the NSPCC does.

Trained **counsellors** work with children and their families to repair the damage caused by abuse and to help them find ways of dealing with their problems. Parents are offered support to become better parents through nurseries, schools and health centres. And the NSPCC also trains and supports teachers and health service workers in ways of helping parents to cope with difficult situations.

Fifteen per cent of 8 to 11-year-olds say that they would not talk to anyone if they had a problem.

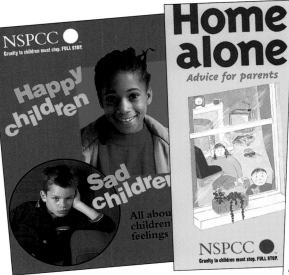

▲ Some of the leaflets and booklets the NSPCC produces offer parents and carers advice about the best ways of caring for children. Some of the leaflets tell people what problems children face and how to take action to help.

▶ The people who work for the NSPCC teams and projects are trained to help children and their parents. They give advice and support to thousands of families every year.

CAMPAIGNING

The NSPCC also uses its special skills and experience to speak out on behalf of all children and young people. This is called campaigning and it is done in lots of different ways. The **charity** produces a range of information booklets and advice materials to give people a better understanding of children's needs. It also helps by getting issues about children into the **media** so that people are more aware of the problems children face. NSPCC staff also **lobby** government **ministers** and **Parliament** to help them find ways of improving laws to help children.

About 350,000 children live in uncaring families who seem to do nothing but criticize them.

MEET CATHERINE HOWARD
EDUCATIONAL ADVISER

I'm the NSPCC Regional Education Adviser for the Midlands. My job is to work with teachers, children, parents and others to make sure that young people of all ages are safe and happy. Part of my work is about keeping children safe from **abuse**. I train teachers and other staff in schools to listen to children and help them. I like my job because I work with young people of all ages and I can focus on issues that I think are really important. Who is going to do their best at school if they are being bullied or abused?

7.30am My first meeting today is at a school about 100 kilometres away, so I leave home early.

9am The Head wants me to help her set up a **peer** support programme. Children are trained to help others if they are unhappy or being bullied. Today we are deciding how to choose the children who will be trained. We agree to interview all those who have filled in an application form.

11.30am I return to the office for any messages. I am working on a leaflet about bullying to help children going to secondary school. I decide what ideas and illustrations I'd like to include.

▼ **Milly, the computerized baby, gives out loud and lifelike cries at random times, day and night. She can even give a report on how she's been treated! Most pupils say that they never realized how hard having a baby was until they looked after Milly.**

Each week around 450,000 children are bullied at school.

1pm I drive to another school to meet the children who are going to work with Milly, our computerized baby. I go over the rules for looking after her. I want the children to learn that having a baby is a big responsibility and a lot of hard work.

3.30pm I talk with the teachers about the ways in which we will organize the class tomorrow. The teacher offers me a cup of coffee and a chocolate biscuit, which is wonderful because I missed lunch again today.

5pm Before going home, I return to the office to collect the training packs I'll need tomorrow and deal with any remaining messages.

▲ **The head teacher and I interview anyone who filled out an application form for the peer support programme. We're delighted that so many want to be involved.**

▼ **Sometimes I'm asked for advice about bullying. Bullying can be really hurtful and it should always be stopped. Anyone who is bullied should tell their teacher, parents or adults they live with. Most teachers are used to handling bullying and should be able to help.**

11

Each year an NSPCC educational adviser contacts 40,000 children with the NSPCC anti-bullying leaflet.

MEET JENNIE GREENAWAY

HELPLINE COUNSELLOR

'I wish there was someone to talk to.' Have you ever felt like this? There are lots of mums and dads, neighbours, children and young people who feel sad or worried and who wish they had someone who would listen and help them decide how to make a difference.

That's where I come in – I'm a telephone **counsellor** with the NSPCC National Child Protection Helpline. It's free to call the Helpline so anybody can ring and talk to us. Counsellors are ready to answer the telephone all the time. I work during the day and some counsellors are here during the night and even on Christmas day, too!

When I talk to people on the Helpline, I do my best to help the children involved. It's important that children feel safe and happy in their families, so that they know how to be good mums and dads when they grow up.

8am I arrive at the Helpline. Two bleary-eyed counsellors who have been working all night are very pleased to see me so they can go home to bed.

8.15am My first call is a mum. She sounds cross because Ben won't go to school. I can hear a baby crying. I listen to Mum and then I talk to Ben. He says he is being bullied at school. I tell him that's not OK and he agrees to go to school while Mum sorts the problem out with his teacher.

9am Another caller is worried about a baby who lives next door. I think a **social worker** should visit the baby and the caller tells me the address. I call the **social services** and they promise to arrange for a social worker to visit.

On average, the NSPCC responds to over 6500 requests for help every month.

10.15am I take a call on the Minicom from a deaf child, who types her message to me. She wants to go to a special club for deaf children. We 'talk' to each other by typing and reading and she agrees to talk to her mum about how she is feeling.

▼ **The Minicom is great way for deaf children and family members to communicate with us. We can have a conversation by writing our questions and answers to each other.**

12 noon I have lots of telephone calls all afternoon about children and their families. Sometimes I ask social services to arrange to see the family, and sometimes the caller decides what to do about the problem themselves.

4.30pm It's time for me to go home. Some other counsellors have arrived now so I know that anyone who telephones us will have someone to talk to even when I'm not there.

▲ **As telephone counsellors we never visit people. We contact social services or other organizations if and when the callers request further help, or if we feel it's an emergency.**

13

The Helpline answers an average of 1400 calls a week from people concerned about children.

MEET JULIE MINNS

PARLIAMENTARY ADVISER

I'm the NSPCC's parliamentary adviser. It's my job to keep an eye on what laws are being passed by the **MPs** who sit in the **House of Commons** and members of the **House of Lords.** I try to improve them to make society even safer for children. MPs are very busy people so it's important that we keep in touch with them so that they're aware of our work. Each month we send out information on various issues, meet with MPs, and arrange questions to be put to **ministers**. That way the protection of children stays on MPs' minds.

9am My first job is to sort through the mounds of paper detailing what's been going on in the House of Commons that's of relevance to the NSPCC. Quite often an MP will have asked a question that gives us information we didn't have before.

10am I meet with our **campaign** development officers to discuss what we want the NSPCC's campaigners to write to their MPs about. We decide to **lobby** on the payment of parental leave for working parents whose children are sick. At the moment many parents lose their pay if they stay home to look after their children.

> There's a huge pile of things to discuss with the campaign development officers today.

14

The House of Commons is part of the British _Parliament_, the country's law-making assembly.

12 noon I have a meeting with Llin Golding MP. Llin has been a keen supporter of our Justice for Children campaign, which aims to make **court** appearances for victims of child **abuse** more bearable. Llin is going to ask the government some questions about the laws on child **witnesses** in the hope they will speed up the changes.

1.30pm I have lunch with a researcher who works for an MP. He helps me keep in touch with what the government is thinking. This means we have a better chance of influencing any plans they have for future laws affecting children.

3.30pm I spend the rest of the day at the office working on a letter about next week's parliamentary **debate**. The debate is about the Health Bill, a law to improve the inspection of **children's homes**, where the most **vulnerable** children live. The letter will be sent to over 350 MPs who support the NSPCC. I hope that some of them will discuss points raised in my letter at the debate.

▲ **The NSPCC helps to protect hundreds of children each year, but that's only possible because the law says it is wrong to hurt children. Every law has to be approved and passed by the House of Commons. That's why it's important for me to keep in touch with MPs.**

There are 150,000 NSPCC campaigners in the UK.

MEET MARGARET McALISTER
FAMILY SUPPORT MANAGER

Sometimes the best way of helping children is by helping their parents. Some parents need support and advice so they know how best to meet their children's needs. In the Northern Ireland region we provide services such as parent groups and after school projects, and we work with individuals as well.

As family support manager it's my job to keep an eye on the various projects in the Greater Belfast area. It's a busy and challenging job and no two days are ever the same. Part of my job is to visit the different projects to check that everything is going well. Today I'm visiting the Clanna family centre in West Belfast.

9.30am The doors of the family centre open and children aged between 2 and 8 and their parents start to arrive. We get out the toys and craft materials for the morning visitors. The activities have been specially designed to help the individual children coming today.

11am It's break-time. The children have a rest and a snack of toast and fruit. Then it's back to the serious business of learning through play. Sand and water, art and craft, songs and rhymes — it's an action-packed session!

While the children play, mums have a chance to talk about any problems they have in a comfy, relaxed setting. They also have the chance to take classes in healthy eating, adult education, or classes to help them become better parents.

16

12.30pm Most families go home for lunch, but some children stay to eat at the centre. Staff use this quiet time to tidy up and get ready for our afternoon visitors.

2pm The early afternoon session is for toddlers aged between 18 months and 2 years. They play and get the chance to make new friends in the safe, cosy playroom.

3pm In the last part of the day 8 to 11 year olds arrive. They play board games, work on art and craft projects and chat to their friends.

4.30pm It's home-time. Everyone leaves with a 'goodie bag' — works of art they've made or some little buns they've baked. I head back to the office to check on my e-mails again and write up a report of my day.

The outside of the Clanna building may look bleak, but inside it's warm and cosy and the staff are all kind and welcoming.

There are 11 NSPCC family centres in the Greater Belfast area, visited by 350 children and families daily.

WORKING FOR JUSTICE FOR CHILDREN

When an adult deliberately **abuses** a child, they are breaking the law. When the police are told about someone breaking the law, that person may have to go to **court**. Sometimes children who have been abused, or who have seen someone else being abused, are asked to give evidence as a **witness**. Being a witness means telling the court all about what has happened. It is a very important job.

NSPCC workers show children pictures like this of the courtroom so they know what to expect and feel less nervous when they go in. It is important that child witnesses feel comfortable enough in court to be able to tell what happened.

This support worker is talking to a girl about going to court. She is trying to help prepare the girl for court and to reassure her that by being a witness she should be able to stop the abuse she's been suffering from happening again.

The Child Witness Support project was set up in 1994, after the NSPCC's 'Justice for Children' *campaign* began.

YOUNG WITNESSES

Lots of young people go to court as witnesses. For many of them it can be a scary experience. After all, none of us finds it easy to do something new for the first time. The NSPCC trains workers and **volunteers** to help and support young people who have to go to court as witnesses.

Support workers will talk to the child beforehand, to prepare them for the day. They explain what the court looks like, the different people who will be there, and what they need to do as a witness. Support workers answer any questions the child may have and talk about any of the child's fears about being a witness. Afterwards, support workers may visit the children and their families at home. This is a chance to talk about what happened and to find out if they need any further help.

▲ **The NSPCC's 'Justice for Children' campaign aims to make people aware of the urgent need to make going to court less difficult for child witnesses.**

➤ **NSPCC booklets like these explain what happens in court and what witnesses are expected to do. They also give answers to questions that child witnesses often ask about court and help them to remember that other children go through the same thing.**

Over 35,000 children are at risk from abuse and have to be protected by the authorities.

WORK IN FUND-RAISING

Everyone knows that money alone cannot buy happiness. But it can pay for people to help and support a child through tough times. The NSPCC is a **charity**. This means that it relies on gifts of money to pay for all the work it does. Donations like this can enable the NSPCC to give a struggling parent the confidence and skills they need to care for a child properly. Or they can give a damaged child the will to live again when they realize that the **abuse** they are suffering can be stopped.

▲ People are willing to do all sorts of weird and wonderful things to raise money for the NSPCC!

◀ Olympic swimmer Duncan Goodhew supported the BT Swimathon in Leeds. The Swimathon is an annual fund-raising event involving over 40,000 swimmers across the country. In 1999 it donated £1 million to help fund the NSPCC's work for children.

The NSPCC has over 200 fund-raising branches throughout England, Wales and Northern Ireland.

The NSPCC employs staff to help organize fund-raising events, encourage people to become volunteers and persuade companies to help out as well.

VOLUNTEERS

Volunteer fund-raisers play a vital role in the NSPCC's work. Every year over 15,000 people give their time, enthusiasm and effort to help raise money in an amazing variety of ways. In street collections volunteers collect money in NSPCC envelopes from homes in their area. In sponsored events people take on a challenge, such as a marathon bicycle ride. They persuade family, friends and companies to promise to give a certain amount of money for each kilometre they ride. Groups of volunteers may also raise funds by organizing fun events like local fêtes, fashion shows or grand balls. The NSPCC has even been involved in fund-raising film premières.

There are also Young NSPCC Groups, so that children and young people have the chance to help the NSPCC. You have lots of fun and make new friends, as well as feeling a real sense of achievement.

A £60 donation covers the cost of answering about 14 calls to the NSPCC Child Protection Helpline.

WORK IN INVESTIGATIONS

Most adults are kind and caring towards children. But sometimes adults hurt children. It's very hard to tell which adults treat children badly. You certainly can't tell by looking at them. Most children know the adult who is harming or **abusing** them. It might be the child's own parent or step-parent. It might be someone who looks after them outside their own family, like a babysitter, or someone who has an important job.

▼ Social workers from the NSPCC investigations unit are called when there is concern about the safety of a child.

FINDING OUT

The NSPCC gets calls from members of the public and professionals who are worried about a child they know. Perhaps they are worried that an adult is harming the child.

The NSPCC may be asked to investigate. An investigation means that a **social worker** from the NSPCC and a police officer will visit the child and their family. The police officer is specially trained in talking to children and young people. The NSPCC will also work closely with other local agencies.

The cost of running one of the NSPCC Regional Investigation Units is over £150,000 a year.

IT HELPS TO TALK

NSPCC investigation teams put children first. This means they listen to what children and young people have to say about what is happening to them, and how they feel about it. This gives the children a chance to talk about any worries and fears they have. Then the NSPCC worker helps the child to sort out those worries and fears. They may help the child concerned speak to their family or whoever looks after them, telling them how they feel and that they want the abuse to stop. The NSPCC worker helps the parents or carers understand what may have happened so that together they can ensure the child is protected in the future.

◀ **When visiting a child's home with someone from the NSPCC investigations unit, a police officer does not wear a uniform. They want to help the child feel relaxed enough to talk to them.**

▶ **Young children may find it hard to explain what has happened to them. Social workers use toys to help them talk about it. Or they may encourage them to draw pictures to describe how they feel.**

In 2000 there were 11 Regional Investigation Units in the UK.

WORKING WITH PARENTS

Most parents want to do their best for their children. Sometimes, though, things go wrong and these good intentions are undermined. Maybe money is tight, or a parent is sick, alone or out of work. Most of the child **abuse** that happens in the UK is committed by parents or other people who are supposed to be looking after the child – the very people the child should be able to trust the most. The NSPCC works with parents in lots of different ways to give them the support they need to become better parents. This helps them to give their children the love and care they deserve.

Some parents don't know how to cope with their children. NSPCC workers in family support services can offer parents guidance and advice on how to give children the love, security and attention they need.

In 1998–1999 the NSPCC helped 1986 families give their children the understanding and care they need.

Having a new baby is both a joyful and stressful time for new parents. The NSPCC provides booklets and support for new mums and dads. They give practical information about how to care for babies and how to ask for extra help if and when it is needed.

Young children have a great time at NSPCC family centres. They can paint, learn, play and read in a warm and bright playroom. If there are difficulties at home, family centres can provide a welcome break for children and their parents.

Every year the NSPCC spends around £85,000 on producing advice leaflets for parents.

EVE'S STORY

When someone is worried that a child is being **neglected**, it can be hard to know what to do. But talking about their concerns to someone experienced can help them make the right decision. It was very difficult for Betty to call the NSPCC Child Protection Helpline, but she knew she had to.

Betty was afraid that her daughter, Jo, was not caring well for her baby, Eve. Sores on Eve's bottom were becoming infected. She had been left on a high bed without anything to stop her falling off, while Jo watched TV downstairs. Jo wouldn't talk to Betty about her problems because they had fallen out, and Jo felt she should be coping on her own. Betty finally called the NSPCC because Jo was planning to move in with a friend, and Betty was worried about her granddaughter's safety.

Betty phoned the Helpline because she knew that the NSPCC would help her daughter, Jo, and her granddaughter, Eve.

A donation of £30 enables an NSPCC telephone *counsellor* to help a concerned caller.

A BABY'S NEEDS

NSPCC staff got in touch with **social services** right away. They worked with Jo to help her understand her baby's needs and how to keep her safe. Jo learnt how to cook healthy foods, to bathe Eve and change her nappy regularly, and how to look after her if she becomes ill. Jo and Eve have now moved into special parent and child lodgings, where a family carer visits every day to help them. Jo is happier and more confident now that she feels she knows what she is doing, and Eve is happier too.

When the *social worker* called, Jo was relieved to get some practical advice and support. The social worker also reassured Jo that all mums find it tough to cope sometimes, and that it's OK to ask for help.

Now Jo feels much happier. She is grateful to Betty for stepping in and these days she's glad to accept Betty's support. Having gained more confidence, she is able to enjoy baby Eve and give her all the love and care she needs.

27

The NSPCC is working with almost 100,000 individual children.

VISION FOR THE FUTURE

The NSPCC's vision for the future is a society where all children are loved, valued, and given the chance to grow and learn. The NSPCC wants everyone – children, parents, teachers, employers, **ministers** and anyone who works with children – to work together to end cruelty to children and to give them the lives they deserve.

Wear the badge. FULL STOP.

FOR MORE INFORMATION CALL 0845 6000 766
Cruelty to children must stop. FULL STOP ● NSPCC

▼ The FULL STOP Campaign got off to a great start. In this picture of the launch you can see Prime Minister Tony Blair, Emma Bunton (Baby Spice) and The Duke of York in front of a huge poster covered with the signatures of those who offered their support.

▲ We know that child *abuse* is still a horrible reality for many children today. Yet we also know that most child cruelty can be stopped – it's just a case of making it happen. The NSPCC FULL STOP *Campaign* is calling upon everyone to help to end cruelty to children.

NSPCC ●
Cruelty to children must stop. FULL STO

I promise to do all I can to help stop cruelty to children

Over half a million people have signed the FULL STOP pledge promising to do all they can to stop cruelty to children.

In March 1999 the NSPCC began a campaign to achieve this goal. It is called the FULL STOP Campaign and its aim is to bring about a major change in society's attitudes and behaviour towards children. The NSPCC wants everyone, everywhere to recognize that cruelty to children is unacceptable and that everyone has a responsibility to protect children. The NSPCC's vision for the future is to have made cruelty to children a thing of the past.

In the future the NSPCC will be offering children even more help, advice and services through working with families, schools and local communities, and through the internet and other *media*.

The NSPCC is always on the lookout for new ways of helping children using new technology. This is the homepage from the NSPCC website on the internet.

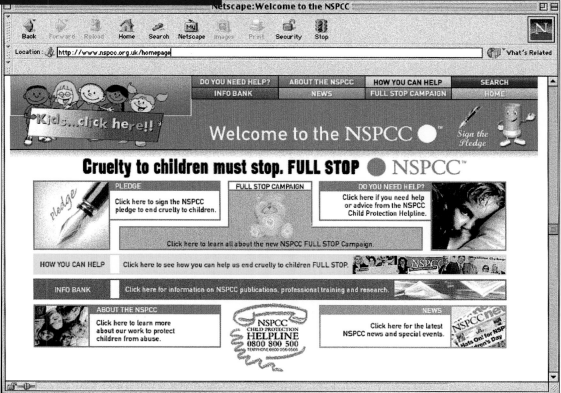

The NSPCC aims to raise £250 million to fund the FULL STOP Campaign.

FIND OUT MORE

If you want to find out more about the NSPCC, read *So What Does the NSPCC Do?* This free booklet is available from the NSPCC Publications and Information Unit.

Publications and Information Unit
NSPCC National Centre
42 Curtain Road
London EC2A 3NH
Telephone: 020 7825 2775
Fax: 020 7825 2525
You can also visit the NSPCC website on: www.nspcc.org.uk
Or e-mail us on: infounit@nspcc.org.uk

You can get many other publications from there too. The NSPCC operates throughout the UK except in Scotland where there is a separate organization, 'Children 1st' (the Royal Scottish Society for the Prevention of Cruelty to Children, 41 Polwarth Terrace, Edinburgh EH11 1NY. Telephone 0131 337 8539).

ChildLine is a telephone helpline for children and young people, and can help with any kind of problem, including child **abuse**. You can also ring them if you are worried about a friend. The number is 0800 1111.You can also write to them at Freepost 1111, London N1 OBR. You don't need a stamp.

▲ **Is it happening to you? If you think a parent or other adult is being unkind and making you feel bad, or if you are worried about a friend, tell an adult you trust. Or you can phone the Helpline for advice – you can call anytime, day or night, and the calls are free.**

The NSPCC Child Protection Helpline is a free, 24-hour service which provides **counselling**, information and advice to adults and anyone else concerned about a child at risk of abuse. If you are a concerned child or young person yourself you can call 0800 800 500 or Textphone 0800 056 0566.

Sometimes children worry that they will be taken away if they tell someone that they are being abused at home. This hardly ever happens. Children are only taken away from home if it is dangerous for them to stay there. Most return home, just as soon as it is felt they will be safe.

The London investigation team interviews over 100 children a year.

GLOSSARY

abuse emotional or physical cruelty. Sexual abuse is when a child is being 'used' sexually by an adult.

Act of Parliament law made by Parliament

campaign/campaigning activities to bring about change

charity non-profit-making organization set up to help people in need

children's homes place for children to live who need care or somewhere to live

commissioner independent person appointed by a government group to do a specific job

counselling talking to someone who is trained to help with your problems

counsellors people who listen to people talk about their problems and sometimes offer advice and guidance

court place where people accused of a crime go to be judged

debate discuss an important issue

House of Commons part of the United Kingdom Parliament which contains elected Members of Parliament (MPs), who make the laws

House of Lords part of the United Kingdom Parliament. Members of the House of Lords inherit their place or are appointed by the Queen.

lobby/lobbying meeting or writing to powerful people to persuade them to make changes to laws and policies

media newspapers, magazines, radio, television, advertising, satellite and other forms of communication

ministers politicians who are chosen to work in the government

MPs Members of Parliament – politicians who are elected to represent local people

neglect when a child's basic needs for warmth, food, etc. are not met

Parliament elected body of politicians who make our country's laws

peer someone who is the same age and from the same background as you

rights children's rights include the right to life, good health, a name and identity, and protection from abuse and neglect. Children also have the right to have their views taken into account.

social services services provided by the government for people in the community who face difficulties and problems

social workers people trained to help and support people

volunteers people who work without being paid

vulnerable easily harmed or hurt

witnesses people who know something about an event and can give information about it

INDEX